Mind Games

A Collection of Thinking Games

Bernadette Kelly

CELEBRATION PRESS
Pearson Learning Group

CONTENTS

Connect the Dot Games

DON'T CROSS THE LINE

This game seems simple, but get ready for a challenge!

You Will Need

➔ pencils

➔ a sheet of paper

Number of Players

➔ two or more

Time

➔ 5–20 minutes

How to Play

Draw ten to twenty dots anywhere on the paper. Take turns to draw a straight line or a curved line from one dot to another. Your line cannot cross another line or pass through a dot. Only three lines may lead from each dot. The player who draws the last possible line wins. The more dots you start with, the longer the game.

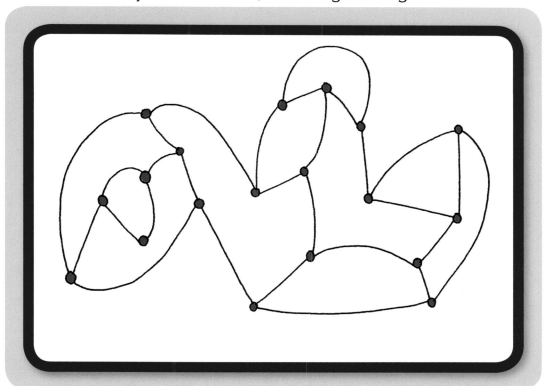

THE SNAKE

Beware of snakebite!

You Will Need

→ pencils

→ a sheet of graph paper with dots drawn at each corner, or paper with a ten-dot x ten-dot grid

Number of Players

→ two

Time

→ 10 minutes

How to Play

Player 1 starts at any point on the grid and draws a connecting line between two dots, horizontally or vertically. Player 2 connects either end of the line to a new dot. Players take turns to connect the lines, creating a winding snake across the grid. The line must not branch, cross, or double back on a line already made.

The person who connects either end of the snake to itself loses the game.

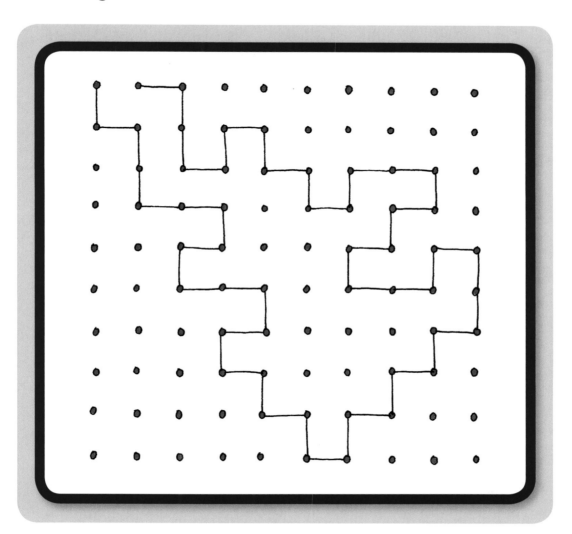

BOXES

Who can claim the most squares?

You Will Need

→ pencils

→ a sheet of graph paper with dots drawn at each corner, or paper with a ten-dot x ten-dot grid

Number of Players

→ two or more

Time

→ 30 minutes

How to Play

Starting at any point on the grid, each player in turn draws a connecting line between two dots, either vertically or horizontally. The player who closes the fourth side of a square writes his or her initial inside and takes another turn. The game is over when no more lines can be drawn.

The player with the most squares wins.

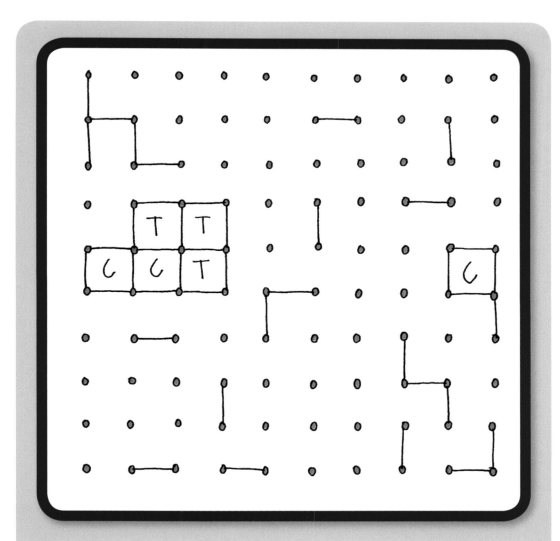

Variation

You can also try playing Triangles using a triangular grid.

INSTANT RECALL

This is a memory game to get you thinking.

You Will Need

→ a tray

→ 10 small objects; for example, a comb, a key, a hairbrush, a ball, an eraser

→ pencils

→ paper for each player

→ a judge

Number of Players

→ small to large groups

Time

→ 5–15 minutes

How to Play

The judge arranges the objects on the tray. Players have thirty seconds to memorize the objects before the tray is removed from sight. Players then have two minutes to write down as many objects as they can remember. The winner is the one who remembers the most objects.

Test yourself now. Memorize all the objects on the tray in the picture below for thirty seconds. Close the book and write down as many as you can remember.

Variation

Use textured objects and blindfold everyone. As well as remembering, players must also guess the objects by touch.

WORLD TRIP

This is a double challenge of memory and geography.

Number of Players

➔ small to large groups

Time

➔ 5–30 minutes

How to Play

Players form a circle. Someone begins by saying "On my world trip I visited . . ." The player names a country. The next player must repeat the country named, and name a country he or she "visited" and so on around the circle. Each turn becomes harder with more countries to remember. You're out if you cannot repeat the countries in the correct order or name a new country. The winner is the last player to correctly name all the countries.

You might find it useful to have a judge write down each of the countries named.

What was that place again?

Variation

Players could also say what they bought in the country they visited. This gives them two things to remember each time. For example, "On my world trip I visited . . . and I bought . . ."

GUESS WHO?

Can you figure out who the mystery character is?

Number of Players

→ small to large groups

Time

→ 30 minutes to 1 hour

How to Play

One player thinks of a famous person or book character. It should be someone well known. This player tells the others the famous person's initials. The other players must guess who the person is by asking questions, which can only be answered with *yes* or *no*.

The player who asks the question that reveals the mystery name is the winner. This player chooses the next famous person or character.

Can You Guess the Mystery Character?

Here are the initials of the mystery characters and the answers to seven questions. See if you can figure out who the characters are.

Character's initials: HG	
Is it a male?	No
Is it a real person?	No
Is it a character in a book?	Yes
Is it a character in a film?	Yes
Is it a good character?	Yes
Is the character a child?	Yes
Does the character have any special powers?	Yes

Character's initials: PP	
Is it a male?	Yes
Is it a real person?	No
Is it a character in a book?	Yes
Is it a character in a film?	Yes
Is it a good character?	Yes
Is the character an adult?	No
Does the character have any special powers?	Yes

Variation

If you only have ten minutes to play, you could take turns guessing students in your class or teachers and staff at your school. Don't use initials—it would be too easy!

Answers on page 24

STAIRWAY

Build a staircase of words to win this game.

You Will Need

⮕ pencils

⮕ paper for each player

Number of Players

⮕ two or more

Time

⮕ 10 minutes

How to Play

Choose a letter. You have five minutes to form a stairway of words beginning with that letter, followed by a two-letter word, then a three-letter word, and so on. The winner is the player who can form the highest stairway.

```
A
A N
A N D
A R C H
A B O U T
A C H I N G
A R C H E R Y
A C R O B A T S
A U S T R A L I A
```

Variation

Start with a three-letter word spaced out across the page. Beneath each letter, write a two-letter word beginning with the letter above. Keep going, adding a letter to each row until you've formed three pyramids. How many words can you come up with in three minutes?

```
    A              N              D
   AN             NO             DO
  AND            NOT            DOT
 ANDY           NOTE           DOTE
```

ACROSTIC MESSAGES

This game uses your imagination—and it's good for a laugh too.

You Will Need

→ pencils

→ paper for each player

Number of Players

→ small groups

Time

→ 5–20 minutes

How to Play

Choose a player's name. Using each letter as the first letter for a word, players each make up a message. **Josie** could become "**J**ogging **o**n **S**aturday **i**n **E**thiopia." **Danny** could become "**D**anger **a**t **N**annie's **n**ightclub **y**esterday." The winner is the player with either the silliest or most sensible message.

Work out who this is:

Inside this inner space you open up.

Answer on page 24

Variation

A player thinks of a place in which treasure is hidden and makes up a coded message to say where it is. The first player to guess the answer wins. For example, "**M**ervin **y**elled, '**B**ring **a g**orilla'" is *my bag*.

Work out where this treasure is hidden:

Ingrid **n**odded **t**o **H**oward.
Each **b**rought **i**mpressive **n**ews.

Answer on page 24

CONSEQUENCES

How silly can a story get?

You Will Need

→ pencils

→ paper

Number of Players

→ small or large groups

Time

→ 10 minutes

How to Play

Each player writes down a part of the story and then folds the paper like a fan to hide what they have written. The sheet is passed to the next player on the left. This is what the players write:

1. a famous person's name
2. who the famous person meets
3. where they met
4. what the famous person says to the other person
5. what the reply is
6. what the famous person does
7. what the other person does
8. the last line is the consequence.

The paper is opened to reveal the story.

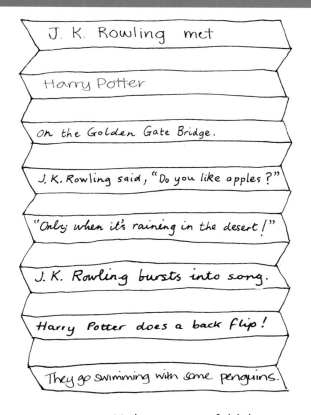

J. K. Rowling met

Harry Potter

on the Golden Gate Bridge.

J. K. Rowling said, "Do you like apples?"

"Only when it's raining in the desert!"

J. K. Rowling bursts into song.

Harry Potter does a back flip!

They go swimming with some penguins.

Make sure you fold the paper like a fan
so everything is written on the same side.

Variation

The game can be played with pictures instead of words.
One person draws the head, the next the body, and so on.

CATEGORIES

This game tests your word skills.

You Will Need

→ pencils

→ paper for each player

Number of Players

→ two or more

Time

→ 10–30 minutes

How to Play

   Players choose a list of categories, such as animals, countries, singers, kitchen utensils, and so on. The aim is to think of as many words as you can that fit the category and begin with a chosen letter of the alphabet. Set a time limit of two minutes. A point is scored for every word, with two points if nobody else has that word.
A new letter or new category is chosen for each round.

Can you add to these lists?

Animals	Countries	Kitchen Utensils
bear	Bolivia	bowl
bee	Bahamas	bottle opener

Here are some categories you might like to choose:

sports

foods

makes of cars

birds

cities

jobs

languages

flowers

Greek and Roman gods

games

Answers

p. 15   Hermione Granger and Peter Pan

p. 19   It is you.

p. 19   in the bin

Index